Pianoworks
Collection 2

compiled and arranged by
Janet and Alan Bullard

MUSIC DEPARTMENT

OXFORD
UNIVERSITY PRESS

OXFORD
UNIVERSITY PRESS

Great Clarendon Street, Oxford OX2 6DP, England
198 Madison Avenue, New York, NY 10016, USA

Oxford University Press is a department of the University of Oxford.
It furthers the University's aim of excellence in research, scholarship,
and education by publishing worldwide

Oxford is a registered trademark of Oxford University Press
in the UK and in certain other countries

First published 2008

12

ISBN 978–0–19–336006–8

Music and text origination by
Barnes Music Engraving Ltd., East Sussex.
Printed in Great Britain on acid-free paper by
Halstan & Co. Ltd., Amersham, Bucks.

Contents

Pastime with good company

Henry VIII (1491–1547)
arr. editors

King Henry VIII was a keen amateur composer, and this song (also known as 'The King's Ballad') became very popular throughout the kingdom. Praising conviviality and comradeship, it includes the lines 'For idleness is chief mistress of vices all: Then who can say, but mirth and play, is best of all?'.

La donna è mobile
from *Rigoletto*

Giuseppe Verdi (1813–1901)
arr. editors

This popular showpiece for the tenor voice comes from Verdi's opera *Rigoletto*. Play it with a twinkle in your eye and a sense of humour as the Duke drinks, shuffles the pack of cards, and sings 'Women are fickle . . .'.

Air

Henry Purcell
(*c*.1659–95)

'Air' is another word for 'song', and this solo harpsichord piece, by a composer particularly noted for his characterful vocal music, has a song-like quality that can be emphasized by expressive shaping of the phrases.

Peacherine Rag

Scott Joplin (c.1867–1917)
arr. editors

Joplin, who worked mostly in St Louis, USA, was the first composer to publish and popularize syncopated ragtime music. *Peacherine Rag* was published in 1901, shortly before Joplin wrote *The Entertainer*. (A peacherine is a cross between a peach and a nectarine.)

Heidenröslein

Franz Schubert (1797–1828)
arr. editors

Moderato

Schubert is renowned for his vocal writing, and he composed over 600 songs in his short lifetime. *Heidenröslein* is a setting of a poem by Goethe about a boy who picks a meadow-rose and is stung for his pains—though finally the rose suffers more. It should be played with simplicity and clarity.

Poor wandering one
from *The Pirates of Penzance*

Arthur Sullivan (1842–1900)
arr. editors

Waltz tempo

Gilbert and Sullivan's perennially popular *The Pirates of Penzance* contains many great tunes. In this song the beautiful Mabel takes pity on the handsome pirate Frederic, to the consternation (and secret admiration) of her female friends.

Adagio
from Sonatina in C

Daniel Steibelt
(1765–1823)

Steibelt was a German composer and pianist who wrote several operas and over 160 piano sonatas. He had a reputation for being vain, extravagant, and dishonest, but the brilliance and colour of his playing captivated his audiences. This Adagio (from his Sonatina in C) calls for expressive phrasing and a sense of conversation between the hands in bars 17–24.

Whatever

Janet Bullard

This piece uses swing rhythm to create a flowing melodic line. As with all jazz styles, the pulse needs to be kept absolutely steady to allow the syncopations to come across. Make the last bar as quiet and cheeky as you can!

The water is wide

Trad. folk song
arr. editors

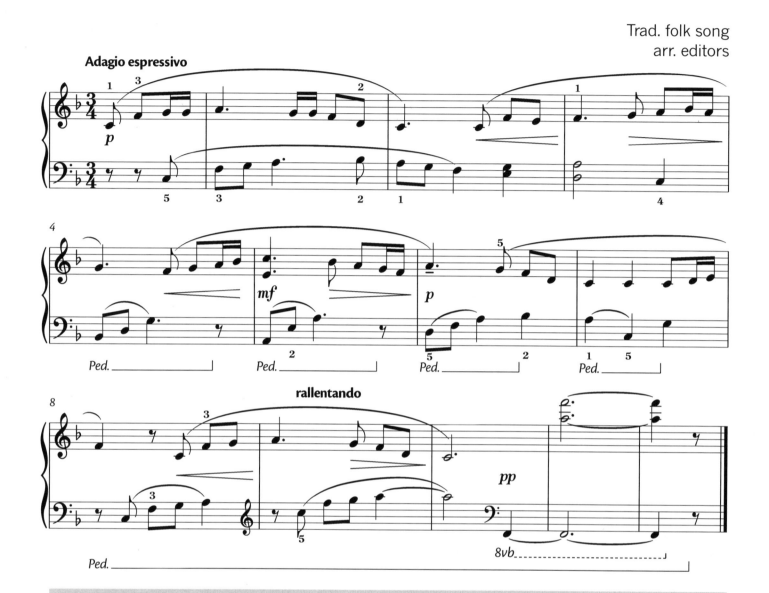

Often known as 'O Waly Waly' ('O woe is me'), this beautiful folk song dates back to the seventeenth century and is possibly of Scots origin, though it soon became well known throughout the British Isles and America. The words of the last verse are: 'O love is handsome and love is fine, And love's a jewel when it is new; But when it is old, it groweth cold, And fades away like morning dew'. The last few bars of this arrangement echo the final words of this verse.

Liberty Bell

John Philip Sousa (1854–1932)
arr. editors

Cast in London in the Whitechapel Bell Foundry in 1745 and shipped out to Pennsylvania, USA, the 'Liberty Bell' was a symbol of freedom and independence, and later of the anti-slavery movement. Having written this march while on tour with his band, the American composer Sousa was trying to think of a title when he received a letter from his wife saying that their son had just been marching in a Liberty Bell Parade. The piece was named, and its fame was assured.

Danse arabe
from *The Nutcracker*

Pyotr Il'yich Tchaikovsky (1840–93)
arr. editors

Tchaikovsky's ballet *The Nutcracker* contains much evocative music. In this exotic dance the sinuous melodic lines, supported by steady and regular left-hand chords, help to create a hypnotic effect.

Jupiter
from *The Planets*

Gustav Holst (1874–1934)
arr. editors

This music is taken from the fourth movement of the orchestral suite *The Planets*, with which the English composer Holst made his name. The stately theme climbs through the octaves, beginning with the lower strings, then moving into the middle register, and finally (in the repeat section) reaching a triumphant climax with the full orchestra. Aim to create this feeling of progression in your playing.

Le petit-rien

François Couperin
(1668–1733)

Sometimes called 'Couperin le grand' to distinguish him from the many musical members of his family, François Couperin was the leading French composer of his day, and is particularly remembered for his twenty-seven Ordres (or Suites) for harpsichord, each containing a number of short movements with fanciful names. This cheerful piece (literally translated as 'the little nothing') is the final movement of Ordre No. 14, which also includes pieces entitled 'The Nightingale in Love' and 'The Plaintive Warbler'.

He shall feed his flock

from *Messiah*

George Frideric Handel (1685–1759)

arr. editors

Handel took just over three weeks to compose *Messiah*, and today it is one of the most performed and loved works in the choral repertoire. This aria should evoke a feeling of calm contemplation—aim to sustain the right-hand melodic line, creating a relaxed and peaceful mood, without letting the tempo drag.

Allegro
from Sonata in G, Hob. XVI/8

Joseph Haydn
(1732–1809)

This is the final movement of Haydn's Sonata in G of 1770. Like most composers of the eighteenth century (and earlier), Haydn notated only the notes and the rhythms, with few indications as to how they should be played; the lively and cheerful character will be enhanced by the suggested articulations and dynamics.

On the edge

Alan Bullard

Insistent repetition creates a feeling of unease in this piece. Keep the driving rhythm steady (not rushed), with clear accents and dynamic contrast; the varied time signatures mostly suggest quaver beats, and you will find it easiest to count quavers throughout. Hold the pedal on at the end to let the final chord ring joyously through the pause.

Prelude

J. S. Bach
(1685–1750)

This is the first of J. S. Bach's *Six Little Preludes* for harpsichord or clavichord, written for his pupils. The ornaments in bars 9–11 could be omitted, although in Bach's time further embellishments would probably have been added. We have suggested phrasing and dynamics to help give a sense of shape and direction to your performance. Look at bar 14 before setting an appropriate tempo!

Take Five

Paul Desmond (1924–77)
arr. editors

First recorded by the Dave Brubeck Quartet (the composer was the group's saxophonist), this tune rapidly
became a jazz standard and is now performed in many different styles. In this arrangement, the catchy melody
is shared between the hands, and the middle notes of the triplets may be omitted (leaving a pair of quavers) if
desired.

Theme from Symphony No. 6

'Pastoral' Symphony, fifth movement

Ludwig van Beethoven (1770–1827)

arr. editors

Allegretto

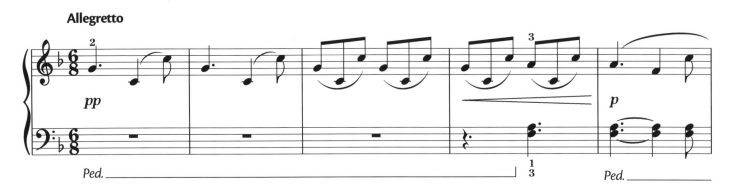

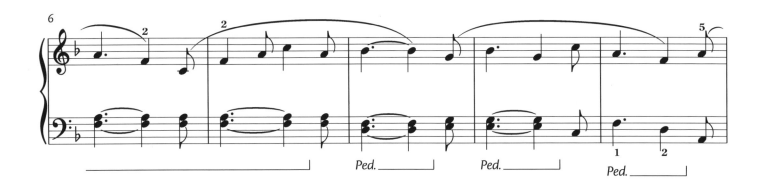

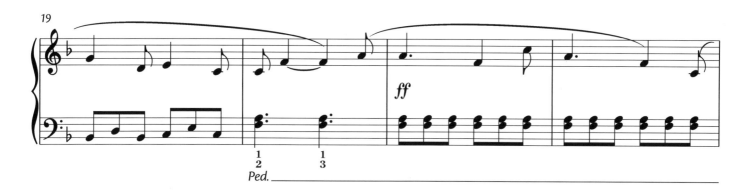

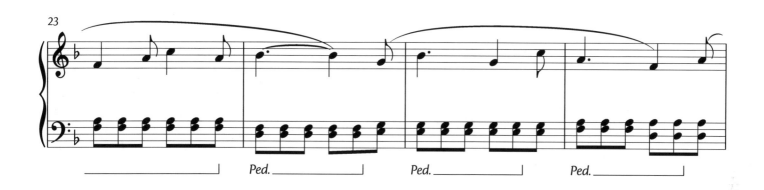

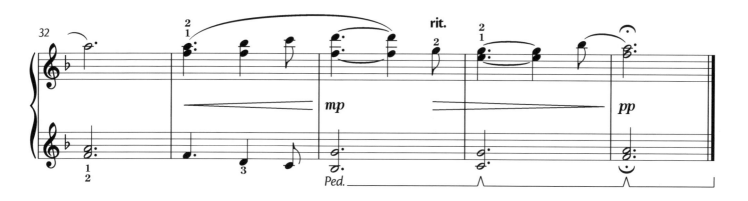

In an age when many composers were happy to enjoy city life, Beethoven was fond of country walks, and the five movements of his 'Pastoral' Symphony depict aspects of life in the countryside—scenes by the stream, merry-making, stormy weather etc. This section from the final movement represents, in Beethoven's translated words, 'the shepherds' song, and feelings of joy and thanksgiving after the storm'.

Prelude

Carl Reinecke
(1824–1910)

Reinecke was a highly respected composer and teacher who became director of the Leipzig Conservatory, and this evocative Prelude is a good example of his elegant and expressive musical style. *Slentando* means the same as *rallentando*.

Sonntag

Johannes Brahms (1833–97)
arr. editors

The words of this song, based on a traditional folk text, explain why Sunday (Sonntag) is the best day of the week—it's the day when the two lovers can meet outside the church gate! Aim to capture the happy optimism of this piece—*nicht zu langsam* ('not too slow') is the composer's marking—while keeping the flow of the melody. In the original version the singer finishes at bar 20 and the piano concludes the song with a graceful postlude.

Là ci darem la mano

from *Don Giovanni*

Wolfgang Amadeus Mozart (1756–91)
arr. editors

This duet ('You'll lay your hand in mine') from Mozart's opera *Don Giovanni* (Don Juan) is sung while the title character seduces the peasant-girl Zerlina. In this arrangement, the music of Don Giovanni is presented in the bass clef, and Zerlina's replies are in the treble. At first she wavers, but then the relationship becomes more confident as the musical phrases get shorter: Don Giovanni sings 'Your heart is mine—confess!', and Zerlina forgets all memories of her fiancé Masseto and goes off arm-in-arm with her new lover. In your performance, follow the dynamic markings with care so that the voice parts come through and the sense of conversation is achieved.

We've only just begun

Roger Nichols
arr. editors

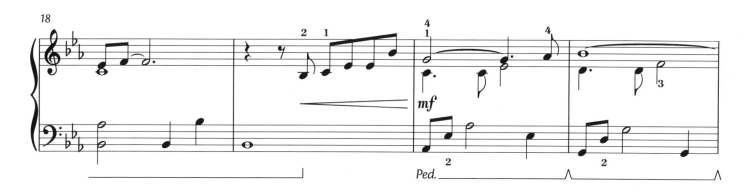

This 'signature' song of The Carpenters portrays a young couple setting out on their life together. With its words by Paul Williams ('We've only just begun to live. White lace and promises, a kiss for luck and we're on our way'), it has become a popular wedding song, and its haunting tune and harmonies achieve an air of timeless serenity.

Flow, my tears

John Dowland (c.1563–1626)
arr. editors

The English composer Dowland was what we would now call a 'singer-songwriter'—he earned his living as a court lutenist in England and Denmark, entertaining courtiers and guests by singing to his own lute accompaniment. (The lute is a predecessor of the guitar.) *Flow, my tears*, which originated as a solo lute piece, the *Lachrimae Pavan*, was one of the most popular compositions of the seventeenth century and appeared in numerous arrangements by other composers all over Europe. Dowland later added the words, which speak of 'tears, sighs, and groans depriving my weary days of all joys'. The heartfelt melancholy of the song echoes Dowland's own reputation as a man given to bouts of deep depression, but also demonstrates his great skill in using melody and harmony to expressive effect. The ornaments are optional.

The Sea is Angry

William Alwyn
(1905–85)

English composer William Alwyn wrote over 60 film scores as well as much symphonic music, and this dramatic work is a vivid piece of scene-painting, using the full range of the piano with colour and excitement.

Sonatina in C
Op. 36, No. 1

I: Allegro

Muzio Clementi
(1752–1832)

II: Andante

III: Vivace

Italian-born Clementi came to England at an early age and earned a reputation as composer, pianist, teacher, and publisher. He undertook many concert tours of Europe, promoting not only his music but also the pianos made by his firm, Clementi and Co. This three-movement Sonatina epitomizes the purity and elegance of the classical piano style condensed into a relatively small-scale piece. The first movement calls for neat finger-work, and the second for expressive and sustained playing (notice that the triplet quavers continue throughout but are not always indicated with a 3). Also in this second movement the harmony can be enriched by holding on the first note of each left hand triplet with the fifth finger, rather than using the sustaining pedal. In the third movement a light and neat touch is needed: steady rhythm is more important than extreme speed.

Scarborough Fair

Trad.
arr. editors

This folk song probably dates back to the sixteenth century and is named after the large summer fair that used to be held at Scarborough in Yorkshire. With its haunting refrain of 'parsley, sage, rosemary, and thyme', it tells of a disappointed lover, and was popularized by Simon and Garfunkel in the 1960s.

Steal Away

American spiritual
arr. editors

One of the most popular American spirituals, *Steal Away* presents a good opportunity for expressive playing. Thinking of the words (below) will bring character to the different phrases: forceful playing with the sustaining pedal held down suggests the thunder of the third line, and then the accents herald the sound of the trumpet at the *Tempo primo*, dying away in echoes in the *ritardando* bars.

Steal away, steal away, steal away to Jesus,
Steal away, steal away home, I ain't got long to stay here.
My Lord he calls me, he calls me by the thunder;
The trumpet sounds within-a my soul, I ain't got long to stay here.

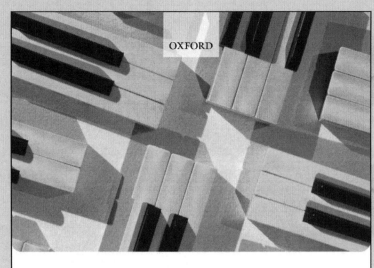

OXFORD

Pianoworks

BOOK 2

WITH CD

Janet and Alan Bullard

A tutor for the older beginner

978-0-19-336007-5

Whether you have a little experience of playing the piano, or would simply like some revision, *Pianoworks Book 2* provides all you need to progress to the next level.

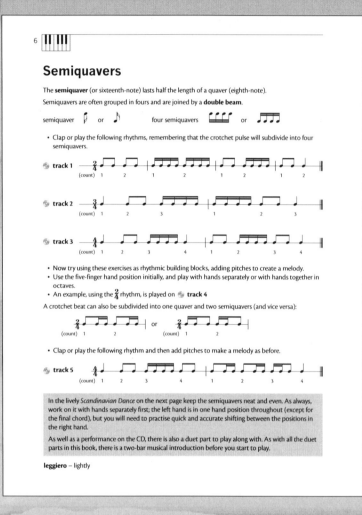

❖ A second tutor book in the Pianoworks series for the older beginner
❖ Well paced, with plenty of examples and exercises
❖ New techniques introduced in a logical progression
❖ Attractive and accessible pieces in a range of styles
❖ Clear and practical layout
❖ CD with performances, backing tracks, and exercises

OXFORD

www.oup.com/uk/music

For the older beginner